PAST IMPERFECT

DAVID OLSEN

Cinnamon Press
:: small miracles from distinctive voices ::

Published by Cinnamon Press
Meirion House
Tanygrisiau
Blaenau Ffestiniog
Gwynedd, LL41 3SU
www.cinnamonpress.com

The right of David Olsen to be identified as author of this work has been asserted by him in accordance with the Copyright, Designs and Patent Act, 1988. Copyright © 2019 David Olsen.
ISBN; 978-1-78864-043-5

British Library Cataloguing in Publication Data. A CIP record for this book can be obtained from the British Library.
All rights reserved. No part of this publication may be reproduced, stored in a retrieval system, or transmitted in any form or by any means, electronic, mechanical, photocopying, recording or otherwise without the prior written permission of the publishers. This book may not be lent, hired out, resold or otherwise disposed of by way of trade in any form of binding or cover other than that in which it is published, without the prior consent of the publishers.

Designed and typeset in Palatino by Cinnamon Press. Printed in Poland.

Cover design by Adam Craig.

Cinnamon Press is represented in the UK by Inpress Ltd and in Wales by the Welsh Books Council.

Acknowledgements

Thanks to the editors of the following magazines and anthologies in which some of these poems first appeared: *Acumen*; *Blueline*; *Cow in the Road*; *Cyclamens and Swords*; *Deronda Review*; *Dream Catcher*; *Earthborne*; *Envoi*; *Frogmore Papers*; *Greatest Hits*, Pudding House Publications; *The Interpreter's House*; *The Journal*; *Journey Planner*, Cinnamon Press; *Literature of Poverty*, World Bank anthology; *London Journal of Fiction*; *Lunar Poetry*; *Lunch Ticket*; *The Nail*; *New World Elegies*, Finishing Line Press; *Pilgrimage*; *Pinyon*; *Plath Profiles*; *Poetry and Business*; *Poetry Connoisseur's Fifty Prizewinning Poems*; *Poetry Salzburg Review*; *Poetry San Francisco*; *Prole*; *Proletarian Poetry*; *The San Jose Journal of Literature and Arts*; *Sentinel Literary Quarterly*; *Skein,* Templar Poetry; *South*; *Turtle Island Quarterly*; *Homeless Not Helpless*, Canterbury Press and *Voices Israel Poetry Anthology 2017*.

Biography

David Olsen's *Unfolding Origami* (80pp, 2015) won the Cinnamon Press Poetry Collection Award. *Past Imperfect* is his second full-length poetry collection from Cinnamon Press. Poetry chapbooks from US publishers are *Exit Wounds* (2017), *Sailing to Atlantis* (2013), *New World Elegies* (2011), and *Greatest Hits* (2001). His work appears in a wide range of anthologies and journals in the UK, Europe, Israel and the US.

A poet and professionally produced playwright with a BA in chemistry from University of California-Berkeley and an MA in creative writing from San Francisco State University, David was formerly an energy economist, management consultant, and performing arts critic. He has lived in Oxford since 2002.

Contents

The Edge of Forgetting
    The Edge of Forgetting   11
    Child's Play   12
    Lovers' Leap   13
    Mother's Hand   14
    Signature   15
    Split Screening   16
    Thick Skin   17
    Redemption Road   18
    Hiking Boots   20
    North Beach Nocturne   21
    Roosevelt Elk   22
    Transatlantic Translations   23
    Private Suite   24
    Sea of Tranquillity   25
    Dark Room   26
    On the Road to Christmas Cove   27
    To a Clock, Sunday Morning   28
    Ashes   29
    Highgate Cemetery   30

Penumbra
    Pathétique   33
    Pawn Takes Rook   34
    Blood Moon   35
    Once More   36
    Minutes   37
    Hollyhocks   38
    Abandoned Night   39
    California Condor   40
    Tumbleweeds   42
    Fracking   43
    Pearls   44
    Horizons   45
    Waking to Wind   46

Available Light
  Black Sun, 1935   49
  Early Sunday Morning, 1930   50
  The Kiss   51
  Plinth   52
  Pont des Amours   53
  Ida Hammershøi's Lament   54
  Wind from the Sea, 1947   55
  Women Alone   56
  Ceiling Fan   57
  Leaving Las Vegas   58
  Roadside Nocturne   59
  Available Light   60
  The Shot   61
  Photographing Pont du Gard   62
  Wildfire   63
  Nocturne   64
  Scrimshander   65
  Moonlight Sonata   66
  Cairn   68
  Hawk Tower   69
  Lighthouse Keeper   70
  Brave Star   71
  Three Seconds   72
  Bones   73
  To Be or Not to Be Macbeth   74
  Poet's Night Out   75
  A Flash of Recognition   76
  Private View   77
  QWERTY   78

No one in the arts succeeds alone.

With love and gratitude to all those who support my efforts and lift my spirits,
including:

Professor Stephen Arkin
Albert Davison Bowers
Byron Richard Brown
Heather & Roger Burt
Hanne Busck-Nielsen
Dr Jan Fortune
Dr Anne Hammond
Dr John Patrick Henry
Olga Myers
Dr Barbara Gail Schonborn
Gwilym Scourfield
Paul Surman
Cathleen Marie Young

Past Imperfect

The Edge of Forgetting
to live with imperfect memory

The Edge of Forgetting

The reach of memory breathes
to the far horizon of fluid self,
a shapeless undulation
of uncertainty, a misted sea
of unreliable recall:
liquid in form, yet vaporous
in transcendent evanescence.

Still, memory's waves persist,
beat upon the strand's
shifting intertidal edge between
the half-forgotten past
and the almost known.

Combers roll toward the shore,
their dissipating force
spent upon a rising beach,
where the overreaching crest
overtakes the hindered foot
and, stumbling, surrenders
itself to inconsequential froth.

Child's Play

At eight or ten I poured coloured marbles
from a doeskin bag onto brown carpet.

The greens in forest cammies were allied
with cavalry blues and arrayed against

commie reds and yellows. I ignored
diplomacy, logistics and the need

for an exit strategy. At my command
a horde of blues and greens prevailed

in glorious conquest, covering
my retreat into presumed innocence.

Lovers' Leap

California

A counsellor at summer camp
taught us how to swim,
beginning with dead man's float
to prove we wouldn't sink,
then added a steamboat kick.
In time we acquired faith
in our buoyant selves,
could jump into the unknown
of black water, and dog-paddle
until we learned the crawl.

One day he led us through
bay laurel and live oak,
manzanita and madrone,
to an overlook. Across
the vale rose a pinnacle
of red rock. Our guide
told of an Indian maiden
forbidden to wed a brave
from a rival tribe.
Less afraid of death
than of life without love,
she climbed the spire
and leapt into the gorge.
Her beloved soon learned
of the sacrifice; in turn
his blood mixed with hers,
which to this day stains the rock.
Chastened elders of both tribes
still lament their shared loss.

Mother's Hand

A teacher's ruler rapped the knuckles
of her left hand to force her to write
with the right. Still, she drew left;

visions conceived in the right
hemisphere emerged through deft
fingertips to her pencil point.

Unlike her sister's careful cursive,
my mother's fluid hand flowed
in an ultramarine rill from the nib.

A few letters are all that remain
of an unwanted third child's script.
She could never be loved enough,

as if in punishment for conception
her knuckles would forever bleed.

Signature

The pen hovers above the document.
Dad wiggles the point to rev his fingers,
set rhythm, or perhaps engage his brain.

H is for Herbert—an unwelcome gift
from parents. *L* is for Leroy—still worse.
The surname's slanted, legible, controlled.
A short, flat line extends the terminal *n*;

this minimal flourish shuns ostentation
but affirms identity, confirms decision.
The commitment's complete, indelible.

Split Screening

Silent home movie

Silvered celluloid
uncoils like fishing line—
a flat monofilament
of unedited bygones.

Retinal memory
integrates stills
to the illusion of smooth
analogue motion.

A cone of light
strikes the bare wall
of a darkened room.
Sprockets click and

disengage. Smoke curls
in eddies of memory as if
trying to retrieve lost words
or recall their meaning.

In three minutes
the reel runs out:
dots polka, then blend
to blinding white

while pupils adapt.
There are no credits,
only blame for Dad's focus
and lack of direction.

Thick Skin

Crazed once-black leather is slack
and languid as a sleeping snake.

The edge is dented where
cowhide strained against
the rear belt loop.

Indigo jeans and sweat
have stained the inside blue.

The hole marking his slim waist
is stretched to a grimace
by the buckle's silent tongue.

Decades ago my dad
showed me how to coil

this belt around my hand,
leaving the brass buckle free
to strike like a whip's tip.

You're never unarmed,
and it will leave scars.

In his belt I recall my father
and the fact of punishment
for some forgotten crime.

Redemption Road

Central Valley, California

The first time I saw cotton
that didn't come out of a blue
Johnson & Johnson box
was alongside Highway 99
near Bakersfield. Kern County
had oil derricks, too, and tall
windmills pumping water
for lonely farms—just like
Dust Bowl photos in old
copies of *Life* magazine.

Throughout a hard drive—
400 dull miles of nowhere—
the windows of our Chevy
were rolled down to allow
whatever cooling was possible
in the hot wind. Afraid
of boiling over, Dad eyed
the temperature gauge.
His arm rested on the sill,
browning in afternoon sun,
a wartime sailor's tattoo
of skull and dice blurring
as ink bled into parched skin.

No radio, little talk, but
a series of five rusting signs
nearly eased the monotony.
Four carried a single line
of witty verse; the last
advertised *Burma Shave*.

Further on, a sign announced:
22 miles to Giant Orange
and, minutes later, another:
13 miles to Giant Orange.
Soon we passed a squat
stand with an orange dome.
They were selling juice—
freshly squeezed and cold.
I whined as Dad drove on
without slowing down. Then:
You have just passed Giant Orange.
Next Giant Orange 26 miles.

And so I came to believe
in second chances.

Hiking Boots

Countless miles of rough terrain
have rounded Vibram lugs
to resemble slumping shoulders
of eroded Brecon slopes.

Granite-ground, scuffed
and creased split-grain cowhide
reveals unresolved skirmishing
between boot and foot.

Which was breaking in the other?
Which yielded at the last?
As I clear my father's house
I come upon these abraded boots,
worn out, yet retained in hopes
of sustaining one more season.

North Beach Nocturne

San Francisco

I set aside a slim volume
from Ferlinghetti's City Lights
and dowse the bedside lamp.

The moist tongue of the night
licks the open window,
softens the room.

Intervals of silence
between burdened groans
of a foghorn's baritone

reveal where the transient
comfort of fog has curled
and bedded for the night—

a sonata for sleep,
composed in blue notes
for Baghdad-by-the-Bay.

Roosevelt Elk

Redwood National Park

I left the Redwood Highway, turned west.
Camping gear jouncing in disarray,
my VW pitched and yawed on the dirt track
between canyon walls draped with ferns.
In the tang of salt I sensed the nearby coast.

The canyon opened onto a meadow
where a herd of elk grazed; I stopped.
Late afternoon sun glinted off golden grass
and tawny hides; heavy breath steamed
the early autumn chill. A park ranger
leaned on a fence edging the meadow,
her strong hands at rest on the top rail.

In silent communion we watched
and at last spoke of the spectacle.
She returned to her pickup truck
and her life of everyday miracles,
I to drudgery and a doomed marriage.
At my car, I glanced up to see the sun
descend into a vermilion sea.

Transatlantic Translations

While flipping through
my guide to European birds,
you suddenly stop.

The Great Northern Diver—
with speckled back,
white breast, dark nape,
and striped collar—resembles
what you know to be a loon.

You reach for your guide
to birds of North America
and compare the Latin names:

Both are *Gavia immer*.

You tell of summers
on a lake in Maine,
learning the language of loons.

You describe mornings
under a zinc-galvanized sky,
your misted sense of sight,
the mingled scents of pine
and coffee, and the call
you can still translate:

Where are you?

Private Suite

Before you knew time, you heard it
without knowing what it was.
It surrounded you like a mist,
had a pulse like yours or hers
or the jellyfish you will see on TV.
It beat faster sometimes, or slower,
but always in patterns—patterns
with regularity but also surprises.
Small patterns repeated and combined,
replicated and divided, grew like you,
folded back on themselves like memory.

Yes. Memory. In time you learned
to recognize the shapes of patterns.
Some pleased you more than others,
but all became familiar, comfortable,
like part of your soft ovoid home.
You learned to expect that something
comes next; you came to think of future.
Before you could conceive of heaven,
you knew that heaven would be
like this, floating in a mist that—
someday—Mummy will call Mozart.

Sea of Tranquillity

Sleepless in my lunacy
I drink the fractured night.
A pearl plump in pregnancy
floats, flaunts its broken light,

sheds its precious tears again—
they ripple off, away—
yet the perfect face remains
benign and beaming, gay;

quicksilver's coalescence
on undulating velvet blue,
its cool luminescence
shining through.

I throw a jagged stone
to scar the mirrored face;
splintering, it comes to one
immortal state of grace.

No brittle crystal, this
reflected liquid light
bestows a silver kiss
upon the lips of night.

Dark Room

The liquid dark seeks its own level,
seeps into the interstices of existence.

Its silence infuses the porous
membrane of mind. The sleepless heart

is heard and rush of blood is felt; so too
the sibilant whisper of every breath.

Silence is neither absence nor void,
but full of the burdensome weight

of memory, and from this dreamless cell
there is no exit, no escape.

On the Road to Christmas Cove

Maine

Like a child impatient for a present,
I hurry past Walpole Meeting House.
Its hoary shingles flake like discarded
scales of a Jurassic hulk

whose spirit refuses to die.
I speed past antique galleries disguised
as tall handsome houses. Not even
the homemade fudge for sale slows

my rush past that smiling girl's drive.
The swing bridge at South Bristol pivots
to cross purposes, allowing a boat
with luffing sails to mock my urgency.

At last I see the point of this beckoning
glaciated finger: there is
something satisfying about going
all the way to the end of a road.

Yet the quick passage of a more
sedate return to Route 1 reveals
a new reflection: the two halves
of a journey retraced need not be equal.

A goal once achieved is easier;
a life remembered, more brief.

To a Clock, Sunday Morning

The salesman, stroking burnished curves,
called you heartbeat of the house
and smiled at this sentimental fool
with plastic card in hand.
He knew which stone to scratch
to find the softest grade
on the hardness scale of life.

Weekly I unlatch your case,
find and fit and turn the key
on a trinity of perfect stems:
one each for strike and time
and Westminster chime—
a note of cultured grace
ensconced on a candled mantelpiece.

Your face, a frosted winter sky,
is rent by two bare twigs:
styli scoring an alloy plate
primed for the acid bath of day,
the balming ink of night.
Your hands move round to pull
the aquatint of time.

Yet there's an end to time:
the tendril of your spring
uncoils its grip on life.
When heart and hours no longer beat
and slender hands are still,
I hope my son remembers then
to seek the hidden key.

Ashes

I kneel on the hearth
and shift the cast-iron grate
to yesterday's news.

My dustpan cannot contain the cloud.
A storm of coughing ensues;
I'm allergic to wood smoke and ash.

The spirit of kindling and oak
has long since escaped up the flue,
and I contemplate the cold remains

of minerals to be scattered somewhere
by a caring someone not yet named
in a testament I should amend.

Highgate Cemetery

London

Adherents are advised
to take the left path to find
the memorial to Marx,
where flowers and candles
daily reproduce themselves
beneath his glowering brow,
and ideas survive the man.

Nearby, standing stones,
crosses and angels erode
in English rain, exfoliate
from freeze and thaw,
their shoulders slumping
from the weight of silence,
exertion of remembering.

Elsewhere, a neglected stone
tilts as the patient movement
of earth undercuts the intended
sense of permanence. Tendrils
of ivy thicken year by year,
embracing the stone inscribed:
In Loving Memory of [illegible]

Penumbra
to sleep in shadows of memory

Pathétique

In momentary glory a negligent star
winks its accidental trace to oblivion.

The full Earth casts a faint glow
upon the new moon's onyx disc,
blots the smudged page of night.

Two bodies complement yet oppose
without relief: one guides tidal affairs;
the other endures without protest
a minor-key *adagio* reprised for fools.

Pawn Takes Rook

They made it all so easy:
those fat and lazy guards,
those flimsy latches.

All this power.
Pitch and roll and yaw—
gentle corrections.

Justice. Their money
shames my brothers
corrupts my sisters.

Sky unbearably blue.
Everything blurred.
Turn. Turn.
Steady. Steady.

Closing fast.
A whore in that window.
God is great
God is—

Blood Moon

Here, in my restive quest for sleep,
northern clouds obscure the sight.

But in cloudless desert skies,
the moon's shaded disc acquires
a third dimension of ruddy fruit
suspended close enough to touch.

When the moon moves beyond
the umbral realm of divided gods,
a memory of blood remains,
distilled to the essence of bone.

Once more

unto the breach, dear friends,
once more, with dubious allies,

summon up the blood
of golden-skinned youth

and loot the gold
of our common wealth

in a cause once reckless,
but now imperative.

Once more, we help men
who shed their kit and ran,

surrendered tools of war,
now turned on us.

Once more, dear friends,
until the next call of destiny

we cannot ignore.
Once more.

Minutes

grey suits expounding
      grey words expressing
           grey thoughts

grey men meaning
      the same monochrome

grey men preening
      round a table   heedless
           of women in black

Hollyhocks

They belonged along the garage wall
until the dilapidated garage itself
came down. Now wayward stems
lack support, sprawl across the walk
like drunks in need of a lamppost.
They meet the definition of a weed—
unwanted here, with nowhere else to go.

Tattered leaves attacked by snails and slugs
are ugly, redeemed only by their blooms.
Five pink petals deepen to a centre
with yellow columnar stamens. In rain
pelted blossoms fall, resemble shuttlecocks
from the neighbour's yard beyond the wall,
like abandoned refugees deprived of means.

Abandoned Night

The half-ghost of my face reflects
in the dark of the carriage window pane.
The night outside seems equally haunted
in the half-light of my view as we pass
an abandoned railway station house.

This place must have been important, once,
to justify stacking bricks course on course,
pouring and paving the platform pier,
erecting and wiring signal lights,
giving work to a man in a blue cap.

All gone now,
but the shell of shabby respectability
in the twilight of what was once
a communal life, half-seen
from a passing train, in passing time.

California Condor

San Francisco, 1987

This man defies all estimates of age,
and seems to have no name, or need of one.
He shuffles, mute, in tongueless tennis shoes,
army surplus coat, and ragged dungarees.
The scraggly beard and hair so nearly match
his sun-scorched skin that his cheeks
trail off into matted fringe that hides his mouth.

With no fixed address, he lives everywhere
and nowhere. He forages The Embarcadero
from China Basin to the Ferry Building.
On good days, the coin-return slots
of newspaper vending racks can yield
a few quarters that missed the lock-boxes.
On good days, he sleeps in the sun
on a concrete bench, his arms flung wide
as if to embrace a tide that has receded
and stranded him, mired in a mud flat
like a worn, discarded tyre.
On good days, stockbrokers and analysts
leave scraps of lunch behind as they return
to their glass castles, having enjoyed the sun
and the fashionable promenade
of trim sailboats on the blue, carefree bay.
For these slim, pretty girls and prosperous men,
there is romance in faraway sights
whose names are crisply spelled on passing ships;
they see the distant mirage, cities of gold
that sparkle beyond the horizon, yet here
the scuttling wharf rat is invisible.

But the bay isn't always benign and blue—
in reflecting a pewter sky, it becomes
the grey-green of serpentine, the crumbling,
faulted rock that underlies the nearby hills.
The wind that ripples the skirt around
that girl's bronzed, untouchable legs in July,
tousles her sun-bleached hair, and turns
the smooth sailboat on its majestic wings,
in December can lash the underground man
and drive him to the shadow of a doorway.
There, in wakeful hibernation, he burrows
for hours, waiting for the storm to blow itself out.

One by one, the old wooden piers burn down.
And progress encroaches on the habitat
of this rough, scavenging bird
that spirals its way in narrowing circles
toward a carcass already picked clean.

Tumbleweeds

West Texas

Depending on the final score,
the week's high or low is Friday night.
The testosterone-fuelled team bus,
boisterous or morose, is trailed home
from an away game by pickup trucks'
blaring horns, or a sombre cortège.
Heroes or goats, the boys return
to face Saturday morning chores
and a small town's joy or grief.

There's little besides football here.
The wooden fronts of frame houses
and the few shops are the colour of dust,
and a boy's outlook is, at best,
tool-pusher, roughneck or roustabout
in oilfields to the south.
Once in a while, a tumbleweed,
blown by desert wind, cartwheels
down the main drag on its way
out of town.

Fracking

North Dakota

A young rancher leans on a fencepost,
squints at a distant horizon as if to discern
the future of his family's land and livelihood.

Prices of open land rise with groundwater
toxicity. Soon neither man nor beast
will inhabit this home on the range.

Columns of stainless steel stab the earth.
Waste gas flares from a pipe;
orange flames corrupt the blameless sky.

Land, once infinite and timeless,
is now utterly changed
by the eroding flood of dollars

created beyond the wounded horizon
by the reckless click of a mouse.

Pearls

Between Harlech and Porthmadog,
three water-colour towns—
a jewelled string of clustered vowels—
hunker in sight of pewter water
and tussock marsh pooled
with eye-of-the-sky. Stunted,
wind-slanted blackthorns erupt
where dry-stone walls confine
sheep tup-marked with blue or red.
A Möbius murmuration
of starlings twists upon itself
in mist above a desert of neglect.
A distant parliament of crows
plucks the eyes of carrion.

Horizons

1.
Bare oak filigrees
engrave the pewter sky.
Each twig obeys genetic dictates
while growing this way or that
at the whim of the wind.
Random yet preordained,
a tree is a fractal struggle
between entropy and destiny
that somehow yields a perfect peace
like the patient lattice
of atoms in a single snowflake.

2.
Poplar skeletons along a ridge
are poised to paint in unison
a blood-hued sunset.
A dogged blaze of hubris
is a self-deluding prelude
to benighted havoc:
an apocalypse of folly.

3.
Our view from the train
renews itself like each passing day,
yet we can't see past
the vain prophecies
called the foreseeable future.
While accident engulfs intent,
we plan and make lists,
heedless of the black swan
beyond the horizon.

Waking to Wind

When whitecaps crested the river's flood
and groundwater seeped like blood
from a saturated dressing,
my battered umbrella's bat wing
sagged, as from a fractured clavicle.
The final score: Gale one, Brolly nil.

Now slanting rain pummels pebbledash,
while the wind's embouchure trills
with rising pitch through the sash,
and curtains sway on windowsills.

Beneath the ragged night's swollen moon,
from sudden gusts or lunacy I wake again
to hear, in my supposed innocence,
the stern reproof to my purblind offence.

Available Light
to preserve memory in creative struggle

Black Sun, 1935

Levee workers, Plaquemines parish, Louisiana

Fourteen Negroes wheel barrows
along narrow planks laid over mud.
They build a levee to prevent
flooding of land they'll never own.
Fearing bites of cottonmouths,
copperheads, and diamondbacks,
they sweat in humid bayou heat.

Arrayed along a nearby ridge,
four white overseers look on
in the shadow of a black sun:
an overexposed disc in an archival print
from a negative mutilated by a hole punch.
Without being told, you and I can guess
we weren't supposed to see this.

Early Sunday Morning, 1930

after Edward Hopper

This sleeping street might lie
in any city neighbourhood
where aching vacancy broods
in grinding times: a pointless
day of rest when few have work.

In tangential sun, no one stirs.
Deflated shadows stretch
from candy-stripe barber pole
and fireplug. Where few can buy,
ground-floor shops are shut.

Shades at upper windows are down,
except where limp curtains hang
in the stagnant air of exhaled secrets
awaiting night, when bare bulbs
expose the slow corrosion of promise.

The Kiss

Pentelic marble, 1901-4, Auguste Rodin (1840-1917)

Dante considered our sin
worthy of Circle Number Two,
but I'd embroidered the tale.
In truth I was reading aloud
of Lancelot and Guinevere
(in hindsight, perhaps unwisely)
when Paolo, overcome by lust,
lost his sense just as my arranged
husband found us in the garden.

The predictable, clichéd result:
a deranged crime of passion.

At first I was grateful to Rodin
for freeing us from this block
of stone, but I've pursed my lips
against this cursed marble's cold
for a hundred years. And poor
Paolo must keep his muscles taut
for all eternity. If enslaved
within eternal bonds, we might
as well endure infernal winds.

Plinth

I endured the chisel's sting
when symbols were incised,
and bits of my rejected self
were chipped and swept away,
reducing me to rough-hewn rock
to make a stable base
and underpin a stately height.

Now, without reward,
I bear a solid weight
with stolid mien,
ignored as passersby admire
the shapely stone above,
its graceful form and sense
beyond my meagre ken.

Pont des Amours

Annecy, French Alps

Shaded by trees overhanging
the centre of an arching span,
she's a slim vision in a long
bridal gown. Slender fingers
clasp a bouquet of white roses.

Whitened skin suggests purity
of Carrara marble, but slowly
her sculpted face turns to smile
at enchanted children; her gloved
hand waves a stately adagio.

When a passerby offers his hand,
she extends fingertips to brush his.
He drifts away; she blows a kiss,
and watches him depart
with wounded longing.

Though this young woman's
a grease-painted actor
busking for coins between roles,
she seems an abandoned bride
destined for unfulfilled desire,

yet keeps a white flame of hope
with the patience of stone.

Ida Hammershøi's Lament

1891. A Paris honeymoon. Oh,
such a romantic time and place!
Vilhelm said I could be his model
and everyone would admire me.

Even after we returned home,
in the early days he sketched me
in charcoal and pencil, but then,
in serious work with proper oils,
I became a mere object in a cold,
sterile house of half-closed doors.

His buyers never saw my eyes.
In so many paintings I faced away,
presented a shapeless back in drab
and frumpy frocks, a black blob
against iceberg walls in the jail
that Strandgade 30 became.

To catch the fading light I had
to pose for hours—keeping still
while he daubed my dress and hair.
I looked out of windows, read,
sat at my writing table or piano—
all the time doing nothing. Once
he painted a vase with greater care;
I was just a blur—a blur
to balance the composition.

Wind from the Sea, 1947

i.m. Andrew Wyeth (1917-2009)

It's not much, really—just an open window
framing a commonplace Maine landscape,
easily dismissed and of no account.
Curtains of faintly patterned gauze with frayed
edges billow in the silent breath of the sea.

Wyeth's tempera palette is equally quiet
and lacking plot; context is all. Beyond
the sash of crippled Christina's attic
dormer, wheel ruts meander through
an ochre field of tawny August grass.

Between the field and a row of gloomy pines,
a stiletto blade of pewter water reflects
a barren sky. The sun, just out of view,
casts a shadow on the sill. A tattered shade
is blown askew and there's a dingy wall.

The scene is outward and within:
the boundary between refreshing space
and stagnant confinement—
the tense border of disclosure
and a veiled secret's trailing edge.

Women Alone

after Vilhelm Hammershøi

Sequestered women, cloistered
in dim austere interiors,
are kept in claustrophobic

solitary confinement. Though
seemingly engaged with tasks,
they're suspended in a frozen

moment of endless domestic
tedium. This one sits reading,
that one writing or sewing,

another is at the piano,
not necessarily playing.
Backs turned or faces averted,

these refined gentlewomen
serve their sentences while
clinging to secret longings.

Ceiling Fan

She, with golden-brown skin
and lustrous dark hair, is here again,
sweetly singing while making the bed
and cleaning the en suite. Unless she
tickles me with her feather duster,
she hardly notices my five
perfectly balanced petal-blades.

My bearings are silent
but I can't refrain from whispering
of all I've seen out of public view.
Gringos who can't afford
air-conditioned resorts fill
the room with bourbon breath,
cheap scent, and the smell of sweat.

The couple staying here now
bicker about everything;
they come in from the bar
and can't even agree on which
of my three speeds they want.
They won't last six months,
if she has the guts to leave.

Leaving Las Vegas

Alluringly slim in slit skirt
and confident in the samba
of her walk, this willowy

chanteuse from Ipanema waits
in a desert of ochre and sage
with a battered leather case

holding everything she owns,
save the gestating remembrance
of that smooth blackjack dealer.

She could face a defeated return
to the roadhouse in Victorville,
but for now she has her looks.

Jaunty and defiant in stance,
she watches the onrushing dust
stirred by a new Cadillac.

She's ready for whoever comes.

Roadside Nocturne

after Edward Hopper's Gas, 1940

In the misbegotten light of a garage lamp,
Pegasus flees in panic from lurking pines
and dreadful dreams aroused by a road
receding into suffocating loneliness.

From urban anonymity to nowhere,
drivers unroll an existential scroll
of futile longing, their missed connections
a map without intersections.

The stiff attendant is like all of Hopper's
figures: never at home in aching shadows
where vacant light penetrates
at sharp angles and no one ever fits.

Available Light

No floods. No fill-in flash.
No aluminised reflector screens.
Just honest light from a window
to brighten her luminous face.
The rest is umbral silence.

Faint shadows in smile lines
recall ripples in Brett Weston's
Oceano dunes at dawn.
Or perhaps the convolutions
in the lava of Salgado's *Genesis*.

Though light guides the eye,
directs its movement through
a manipulated image, it's clear
from Caravaggio's chiaroscuro:
truth inhabits equally the dark.

The Shot

Santiago, 1979

Fixed in grainy silver halide memory,
an unretouched image of stark
black and white emerges from rippling grey.
Brittle, crystalline light from a street lamp
softens, annealed in the mist of Chilean
winter night. Two soldiers in heavy coats
lean against the lamp post, smoking.
Their harmless ruminations contrast
with the cold glint of light on barrels
of automatics slung from slouching
shoulders.

                I have Tri-X in my camera
and light enough to yield a tonal range
from glaring white to deepest black:
a sharp vignette with focus on steel.

Nearby, from under mascara
the vacant eyes of shattered
windows stare; the burnt-out
face of Allende's palace is pocked
by bullet marks.

Wary of shutter's snap,
unable to explain I mean no harm,
in fear I leave my film untouched by light
and scuttle into the anonymous night.

Photographing Pont du Gard

After driving through villages
and vineyards to view for myself
this Roman aqueduct—depicted
in my schoolbook—I look up, up
to three tiers of arches supporting
the ancient watercourse to Nîmes.

I climb to the wide walkway,
but while others stride to the centre
of the span, and still braver souls
ascend to the third level, I dare
only far enough to stand yards
from the parapet and snap
the Gardon River below.

Unable to match the placid solidity
of these honeyed stones, I wobble
back to the comfort of *terra firma*,
driven by the imperative of vertigo.
And while others venture
to the edge of the gorge beyond
the bridge, I adhere to the path,

where overgrown vantage points
offer only obstructed views. Though
clear postcard shots are beyond me,
I frame the bridge between two trees:
one leaning left, the other right.
They form a perfect V—*quinque*—five.

Wildfire

Oil on canvas. Artist unknown. Style of late Goya.

Ochre foreground suggests oats or wheat.
Upper left is cerulean. Banded clouds
with alizarin crimson undersides

dissolve into haze of darkening red.
Middle left is burnt umber and ivory black.
At centre is a wide horizontal swath

of glowing cadmium red edged
with chrome yellow billowing right,
swept by dry westerly wind.

Downwind of char and onrushing flame
is an indistinct squiggle of dark,
perhaps a human figure. Running.

Nocturne

A featureless expanse of midnight blue—
thinly applied monestial or Prussian—
bleeds round the edges of an unframed
square, suggesting a limitless sky.
But if this is night, where are the stars?
Each vaguely possible mote vanishes
when I fix on it. In my urgent search
for comforting light, I'm trying too hard.

Stand back.
                Ignore the card.
                                  Breathe.

Why paint a vacant nothing,
this riddle of squareness?
And why blue ... this darkest blue?
Instead of the cheery cerulean
of a Mediterranean sky, this bruise,
deep as the heart of misery,
conceals lurking primal fears,
summons tears of thwarted desire,
and crushes all hope.

It might just be my wish to find
something, anything, any relief
from this terrifying abandonment,
but inches from the bottom
there seems to be a faint glow
above an indistinct horizontal line.
Beneath it, a hint of uncertain light
ripples toward me. Yes.
Under the bleak near-black sky,
from beyond a sea of doubt
comes the promise of dawn.

Scrimshander

Sleepless below decks, on edge
and annoyed by the humming
breath of slumbering men,
he slips from his hammock,
lumbers up to the rolling deck.

Amid the strum of the breeze
on taut lines, the timbers' creak,
and whispers of water sliding by,
he fishes two objects from his vest.

By the light of a ripened moon,
with his seaman's knife—
meant for cutting cordage—
he engraves an orca's tooth.

At dawn he probes the glass
of a hurricane lamp, and rubs
black into grooves inscribed
in ivory to reveal the scene:

a square-rigger under sail—
the only home he can recall,
wide as the sea itself, and free.

Moonlight Sonata

Children no longer dare to play
among the rampant brambles
beyond that reluctant iron gate.
Their parents say, when clouds
in fury tear across the moon,
in that unbalanced light a woeful
woman's face appears at a window
of that derelict house. The rare
passerby might hear familiar strains
of Beethoven, obsessively played.

Old-timers still speak of the murder
of a concert pianist on the night
of the full moon many years ago.
It was supposed, with near certainty,
that her husband killed the woman
in a crime of passion on discovering
her infidelity with a charismatic violinist.

The presumed killer left town in haste.
Police traced him to Southampton,
but by then a ship had sailed for Australia.
His name did not appear in the manifest;
the trail went cold, the crime unsolved.

On daytime rambles I sometimes pass
by that accursed red-brick Victorian,
but as a retired mining engineer returned
from many years abroad, I've faith
in reason. I'm a man of science, and give
no credence to superstitious claims.

Yet, as I regard my weathered face
and grey beard in the mirror, I confess
to true lunacy: when the fullest moon
opposes the sun, in that intemperate time
I avoid the house. For in those heavy hours
I dread descent into the web of madness.
The haunting's not in that forbidding
house; it's in a fragile mind that clings
to the fraying edge of sanity.

Cairn

      stone
      on stone
      on stone
      on stone
deter the raven

weeping
keening

rite of honour and dignity
quest for eternity
gesture lending the vanity
of permanence
to balance
fragility
of forgiven flesh

eternal stones
weigh upon
bones
of the vast unknown

Hawk Tower

i.m. Robinson Jeffers (1887-1962)

You perch nearby to rest—
barely tame, more nearly wild—
your chin keeps falling to your breast.
Granite father and yet child,
you tire of making every bit
of your aerie come at last
to a balanced perfect fit.
No lyrics soar above the cliff;
all passion's spent in the quest.
We now reflect as if
the sea's looking-glass
reveals two starving things:
you and I—our time having passed—
are hawks with broken wings.

Lighthouse Keeper

i.m. Philip Larkin (1922-85)

Freed of burdensome entanglements
in your high-windowed tower,
you'd have loved the solitude
and simplified arrangement of life.

In your vigil over those in peril,
as tender of Fresnel and lamp,
you'd have probed the menacing
recesses of the night. Alone

with the steady breath of the sea,
each day you'd have added
a fleeting line to the terse litany
of the Shipping Forecast's

transient Beauforts and millibars,
then resumed carving a scrimshaw
of enduring ivory words, while
pondering what remains of us.

Brave Star

for Jen

You sparkle in illuminations,
calligraphy and luminous poems,
while inhabiting constellations
of symptoms, nebulae of syndromes.

You endure the torture inflicted
by blameless, afflicted
bones—every joint insecure,
each a black hole of pain. Yet your

constant courage shines from light
years beyond an unreachable place
somewhere in the indigo night,
bearing all with velvet grace.

Three Seconds

for Weldon Kees, (February 24, 1914 — July 18, 1955?)

Despite discovery of your abandoned car
on the Marin approach to the Golden Gate,
I'd like to think you went to Mexico
and disappeared in verdant hinterlands.

But could you — as film-maker and painter,
photographer and poet with movie-star looks —
have survived the obscurity of silence?

No, you likely straddled the rail,
perhaps to hesitate and contemplate
the folly of the world, then peeled
resisting fingers from the cable strands

and

let

go.

From so far above the tidal surge,
your plunge was faster than a speeding car.
Did you live 3 seconds of perfected clarity?

Or suffer blurred regret at your descent
into the dark currents of your poems,
as you realised their ultimate truth?

Bones

i.m. Sylvia Plath (1932-1963)

the last poems
       incandescent
              spirit distilled to essence

bones without flesh
       bones without marrow
              bleached bones

mineral earth
       coalesced
              dust of broken stars

To Be or Not to Be Macbeth

Whatever possessed me to read for
a minor part: second soldier or page?
I thought to join my buddies on a lark,
but why'd I begin with the Scottish play,
and find myself selected for the lead?
Not yet a man, I must be a warrior-king.

In dress rehearsal everything went wrong.
Everyone knows the curtain shouldn't rise.
But time acquires its own relentless drive,
and people sitting in the dark have paid.

So I'm in the wings with jellied knees—
my entrance and cue await—while lights
are on the witches three. I can't recall
my line. What am I supposed to say?
As from far away, I hear a witch:
Peace! The charm's wound up.

Someone shoves me from behind.
I stumble onstage, blinking in the lights.
I clutch Banquo's arm to hold me up,
and from somewhere unknown to me
comes the missing line. I find my voice:
So foul and fair a day I have not seen.
And so begins my rise and fated fall.

Poet's Night Out

Kiss partner goodnight.
Turn out bedside lamp.
Mime sleep. Think.

Turn on bedside lamp.
Scribble note to self.
Turn off bedside lamp.
Mime sleep. Think.

Turn on bedside lamp.
Scribble note to self.
Turn off bedside lamp.
Mime sleep. Think.

Turn on bedside lamp.
Dodge thrown pillow.
Retrieve spare duvet.
Retreat to sofa. Sulk.

A Flash of Recognition

In a bookshop aspiring
to Ferlinghetti's City Lights,

our eyes meet; we shake hands
before the Great Poet reads.

I tell him I'd attended his course
on a drippy London afternoon

a few years before. I supply
just my forename; I'm so obscure

there's only a quark-sized chance
he'd heard of the rest.

He says I resemble someone else,
whose name is John.

Private View

In other shows, I've marked my
favourite piece NFS—Not for Sale.
It's the perfect expression, the epitome
of who I am, the realisation of how I see.
The work's the culmination of my talent.
It combines vision and technique,
symbol and substance, as my other works
have never done—or may never do.

But for this exhibition I've hung the piece
with tender care, given it prominence
as an offering, my gift to the world.

Yes, the time has come to allow
its separate existence, like a fledgling
pushed from the nest, or a daughter
who's learned all she can from me.
If the piece is sold, I'll not likely
see it again. I'll no longer possess
this confirmation of my identity.

Weaving through champagne flutes
and trays of canapés, the gallery
owner applies a red dot to the frame,
and there's applause—and pride.

But my studio will grieve. The worst
of creation is surrender, the letting go.

QWERTY

From among the Smith-Coronas, Remingtons,
and Royals on dusty display in a charity shop,
I choose an Underwood, and begin a patient search
for a new ribbon—a daunting quest for what
was once a trivial task.

I'm a wannabe Chandler or Hammett with a half-
empty bottle of bourbon, a dirty glass, and
a candlestick phone on a battered wooden desk
with sticky drawers. The filing cabinet's full
of dirty shirts. A shoulder holster with a nickel-
plated .38 hangs from the clothes tree
in the corner.

My going rate's 25 bucks a day plus expenses.
Unless I'm on a case, you can always find me
in my office—south of Market on Howard Street.
I'm waiting for a dangerous dame with great legs
and a slit skirt to saunter through that frosted-
glass door.

The floor's littered with crumpled false starts.
I've typed Chapter One a dozen times, maybe more.
I want to type *clak-clak-clak*, but only manage
clack, clack. Reluctant sentences just beyond
reach evade me.

As fingers pound resistant keys, I hear the *ding*
of a silver bell warning of the approaching
end of the line.